Doggie Styles
Fashionable Dogs Coloring Book

By Lilt Kids Coloring Books

Copyright © 2014 by Lilt House

All rights reserved. This book or any portion thereof may not be reproduced or used in any manner whatsoever without the express written permission of the publisher except for the use of brief quotations in a book review.

This coloring book comes with a free printable pdf version - so you can print another one when the kids are done with this one!

Go to

Liltkids.com/stylish-dogs

to download it.

Made in the USA
San Bernardino, CA
15 August 2016